a gift for:

_____

from:

_____

Published by Hallmark Books, a division of
Hallmark Cards, Inc., Kansas City, MO 64141.
Visit us on the Web at www.Hallmark.com.

Editorial Director: Todd Hafer
Art Director: Kevin Swanson
Designer: Michelle Nicolier
Lettering Artist: Sarah Cole
Production Artist: Dan Horton
Research Assistant: Carrie Bolin

ISBN 978-1-59530-106-2
BOK4329

Printed and bound in China

101 Amazing Things about Love

about Love

GIFT BOOKS
from Hallmark

INTRODUCTION

It seems we humans come standard with state-of-the-art love capabilities. We can give it, take it, feel it, and even steal it. We sing about it, talk about it, write about it. And, yes, sometimes we lose it. But there's one thing we simply can't do—and that's live without it. We love our lovers, our kids, our pets . . . and we live for them to love us back.

But what do you really know about love? Do you know which Beatles love song features a stolen instrument? How Lauren Bacall bade a final farewell to her beloved Humphrey Bogart? Or which U.S. state has the highest male-to-female ratio? How about the anatomy of a kiss? (This is stuff they didn't teach you in high school.)

For anyone looking for love—or at least some of the amazing stories, facts, and legends surrounding it—this book is for you. It's a veritable feast of information about all things romantic, sentimental, or just plain lovely. So sit back, relax, and ponder the ways love can still surprise and delight . . . and amaze.

"Love is a fruit
        in season
at all times,
        and within reach
of every hand.

MOTHER TERESA

LOVE TAKES THE CAKE.

Wedding cake was originally designed to be something that attendees threw at the new bride and groom, just as we toss rice or birdseed today. Fortunately, the projectile-era cake was unfrosted—leaving attendees' fingers (and brides' and grooms' faces and clothing) much less messy.

THOMAS EDISON WAS EVEN INVENTIVE WHEN IT CAME TO LOVE.

Edison, the renowned inventor, and his wife, Mina, used to communicate with each other privately at parties by tapping out Morse code messages onto each other's hands. Edison even used this method to propose to Mina.

"gravitation cannot
be held responsible
for two people
falling in love."

ALBERT EINSTEIN

LOVE DOESN'T ALWAYS PAY,
EVEN IF YOU'RE SHAKESPEARE.

Renowned playwright William Shakespeare was lucky
that he inherited some real estate and garnered
additional income as an actor. The most he ever earned
for writing a play was about eight pounds
(equivalent to about $1,300 in today's U.S. dollars).
In fact, the Bard's annual play-crafting income never
topped 20 pounds (about $3,300). But then again,
perhaps he penned his plays, not for money, but for love.

"*Love comforteth
like sunshine
after rain.*"

WILLIAM SHAKESPEARE

A DETERMINED MUSICIAN WILL BEG, BORROW, OR STEAL TO CREATE A GREAT LOVE SONG.

Pay special attention to the instrumentals next time you listen to the classic Beatles love song "Love Me Do." John Lennon was still a struggling musician when the song was recorded, so he played the harmonica part on an instrument he shoplifted.

LOVE IS FOR THE BIRDS *(really)*.

It was once believed that birds chose their mates for
the year on February 14. Doves are one type of bird
that mate for life, and thus the dove became
a symbol of fidelity and love.

"For love
is heaven,
and heaven
is love."

SIR WALTER SCOTT

LOVE CAN OUTLIVE THE LOVER.

The day after comedian Jack Benny died, a single red rose was delivered to Mary, his wife. Each day after that, another blossom arrived. When Mary investigated the mystery, she learned that her husband had included a provision in his will to have a perfect red rose sent to her—each day for the rest of her life.

BEING A KING DOESN'T MAKE YOU "THE KING OF LOVE."

Henry the Eighth might have enjoyed some success as king of England, but while he could rule a country and face off against the Catholic Church, he was ruled by bad behavior and poor decisions when it came to marriage.

HERE'S A RECAP OF HENRY'S CHECKERED LOVE HISTORY:

The Six Wives of Henry VIII

Catherine of Aragon: Married Henry in 1509. Marriage annulled in 1533.

Anne Boleyn: Married Henry in 1533. Beheaded three years later.

Jane Seymour: Married Henry in 1536. Died a year later.

Anne of Cleves: Married Henry in 1540. Marriage annulled that same year.

Catherine Howard: Married Henry in 1540. Beheaded in 1542.

Catherine Parr: Married Henry in 1543. Survived the marriage, unlike her five predecessors. Most likely because Henry died in 1547.

A GREAT LOVE STORY IS PURE POETRY.

The art of written correspondence has fostered many relationships. So it's no surprise that Victorian poets Robert Browning and Elizabeth Barrett began their courtship through letters in 1845, when Robert wrote to thank Elizabeth for mentioning him in one of her poems. Elizabeth's father forbade her to see Robert, so the two courted through the mail for 20 months. Their letters, numbering almost 600, are among the world's most famous love letters. Robert and Elizabeth ultimately eloped and lived in Italy until Elizabeth died in her husband's arms in 1861.

"So, fall asleep,
love,
loved by me...
for I know love,
and am loved
by thee."

ROBERT BROWNING

LOVE AND CHOCOLATE CAN
BE A DEADLY COMBINATION.

Not long after its introduction in Europe, chocolate's
strong taste was discovered to be a good disguise for
poison. One case of overt poisoning took place in
17th-century Spain, when a reputed "lady of
quality" sought revenge on a lover who had jilted her.
She held him captive in her house, where she gave him
a choice: death by dagger or by poisoned chocolate.
He chose the chocolate, drinking it to the last drop.
He died within the hour, but not before complaining
that the chocolate could have used a bit more sugar.

LINCOLN KNEW LOVE.

Inside the wedding band that Abraham Lincoln gave
Mary Todd were engraved the words "Love is eternal."
When Lincoln, the victim of an assassin's bullet, drew
his last breath, someone in the room said,
"He belongs to the ages."
Mary responded,
"No, he belongs to *me*. Our love is eternal."

"give all
to love;
obey thy
heart."

RALPH WALDO EMERSON

IN LOVE, LIFE CAN IMITATE ART—
JUST ASK BOGEY OR BACALL.

When Humphrey Bogart's death ended his 12-year marriage to Lauren Bacall, Ms. Bacall placed a small whistle in his urn in memory of their first film together, *To Have and Have Not*. In the film, Bacall spoke the now-famous line, "If you need anything, just whistle. You know how to whistle, don't you, Steve? You just put your lips together and blow." The inscription on the whistle she placed in the urn reads, "If you need anything, just whistle."

LOVE MAKES A KNIGHT
DO FRILLY THINGS.

Have you ever wondered why ribbons, lace, and
other frills are traditional wedding decorations?
The custom dates back to the Middle Ages, when
a knight would ride into battle sporting a ribbon
or scarf given to him by his lady fair.
(Incidentally, the word *lace* comes from
a Latin word meaning to "ensnare.")

"Love conquers all."

VIRGIL

NAPOLEON WASN'T SHORT ON LOVE.

Despite putting his couriers in great danger,
Napoleon Bonaparte, the famous diminuative French
general, often took time to pen and send
letters to his beloved Josephine, even while
he was at a battlefront.

*"Love teaches
even asses
to dance."*

FRENCH PROVERB

14

LOVE CONQUERS DISTANCE.

In Old Testament times, the Queen of Sheba was
so intrigued by King Solomon's famed wisdom
that she journeyed from her home country,
located near the southern end of the Arabian
peninsula, to Jerusalem. Upon meeting
Solomon, she peppered him with questions,
like a B.C. game-show host. Solomon answered
even her toughest queries—and showed
her his great wealth.

The queen became one of Solomon's wives.
And, according to legend, a son she had with
Solomon was crowned the first king of Ethiopia.

15

LONG-DISTANCE LOVE
CAN BE VERY, VERY EXPENSIVE.

A 24-year-old man in Denmark found himself
facing jail time for fraud because he was unable to pay
the $117,000 phone bill for calls to his
sweetheart in India.

The lovelorn Dane met his 18-year-old love through
a magazine that publishes names and phone numbers
of people wanting to make long-distance love
connections. And what a connection he made! One
of his calls to Madras, India, lasted 21 hours.

"The course
of true love
never did
run smooth."

William Shakespeare

16

LOVE AND MONEY DON'T MIX WELL.

Some people misquote the Bible, claiming that it says, "Money is the root of all evil." But the real verse, penned by Saint Paul is, "The love of money is the root of all kinds of evil" (1 Timothy 6:10). This ancient wisdom seems to be playing out in the troubled lives of some celebrities. In a nationwide poll, the number one reason Americans gave for young celebrities' troubles was "too much money"— cited by 79 percent of the respondents.

LOVE AND CHESS DON'T MIX SO WELL EITHER.

In 1213, King Ferrand of Portugal was held captive by the Turks for 13 years. His captors demanded a ransom for his release, but Ferrand's queen, Jeanne, refused to pay.

Before he was captured by the Turks, Ferrand and Jeanne had engaged in a spirited game of chess. Jeanne won. Upset, the king punched his wife in the nose. (And you know what they say about paybacks.)

CHOCOLATE——THE STUFF OF LOVE?

For centuries, chocolate was credited with aphrodisiac qualities. In fact, the Aztec emperor Montezuma II always drank chocolate, seasoned with a dash of chili powder, before visiting his harem.

Chocolate's reputation as a love-enhancer continued to grow, and in the 17th century, Johannes Franciscus Rauch, a theologian, condemned chocolate as an "inflamer of passions" and urged monks not to drink it. He even demanded that the use of chocolate be banned in all monasteries and other holy places.

19

LOVE TRUMPS ROYALTY.

Falling in love at first sight, England's Prince Edward
VIII gave up the throne to marry his true love,
American divorcée Wallis Simpson. Edward's decision
was seen as scandalous by the proper royal family,
who ostracized Edward and Wallis. Undaunted,
the couple lived happily together until Edward's
death in 1972.

*"They gave
each other
a smile
with a future
in it."*

RING LARDNER

GIRLS REALLY DO HAVE COOTIES
(but so do boys).

Cooties, that mysterious condition that has hampered many a schoolyard romance, are real. Cooties are lice, parasitic insects who like to dwell on humans—and other warm-blooded creatures. Body lice, the ones commonly called cooties, are truly something to be feared by children and adults alike, as they can spread typhus fever. The term *cootie,* incidentally, might spring from the Malay word kutu, which means "biting insect."

THAT SAYING ABOUT THE WAY TO A MAN'S HEART? TURNS OUT IT'S TRUE.

In Italy's *Siurgus Donigala*, bachelors' hearts truly are reached through their stomachs. Eligible young women make sweet breads in unusual shapes for the region's Feast of the Bachelors. Due to the enormous consumption of bread and wine at the three-day event, there are typically few single people remaining at the end of the festival.

SOME ARTISTS HAVE STRANGE WAYS OF EXPRESSING LOVE.

You've probably heard the tale of artist Vincent Van Gogh slicing off his earlobe, but do you know why? Van Gogh's amateur self-surgery was to impress a girl named Rachel. To display his affection, Van Gogh sent Rachel his severed lobe, along with a note instructing her to "Guard this object carefully." Rachel's reaction? First she fainted. Then she reported the incident to the village constable.

"In our life
there is a single
color,
as on an artist's
palette,
which provides
the meaning
of life and art.
It is the color of love."

MARC CHAGALL

SOME GUYS LOVE THEIR CARS—
WAY TOO MUCH.

When Tennessean Buster Mitchell's girlfriend walked
out on him, the 28-year-old found a new love and
decided to marry her. He visited the county
courthouse in Knoxville and began filling out an
application for a marriage license. He listed his
fiancée's birthplace as Detroit, her father as Henry
Ford, and her blood type as 10 W-40. The clerk
stopped Buster and informed him that one can't
marry his '66 Ford Mustang GT, at least not in
Knoxville, Tennessee. Rumor has it that Buster plans
to try again, perhaps in a county with less
stringent marriage statutes.

24

LOVE IS UNIVERSAL, BUT DATING PRACTICES CERTAINLY AREN'T.

On the island of Trobriand, it is customary for a man to bite off the eyelashes of his lady friend as part of the courting process. However, he would never take her out to dinner unless they were married. On Trobriand, you disgrace a woman by sharing a meal with her before marriage.

KISSING IS SERIOUS BUSINESS; JUST ASK ANY ITALIAN HISTORIAN.

All the casual kissing that goes on today would
have never been tolerated in medieval Italy.
In that setting, kisses weren't taken—
or given—lightly. In fact, if a man and
a woman were seen lip-locking in public,
they could be forced to marry each other.

YOU'VE HEARD ABOUT THE ODD COUPLE, BUT WHAT ABOUT THE ODDS COUPLES?

For a single woman, where's the best place to find a husband? Well, here are a couple of ideas on where *not* to look. The odds are 70 to 1 that you won't marry a guy from the office—and 100 to 1 that you won't marry a supervisor or manager. Also, despite what your mother might wish, it's 1,700 to 1 that you won't marry your doctor.

27

THE PURSUIT OF LOVE CAN TAKE A WOMAN WAY, WAY BEYOND BED, BATH, AND BEYOND.

Today's women enjoy a variety of lotions and potions to use before a big date. But did you ever wonder what women centuries ago used to soften and scent their skin? The ladies of ancient Rome deserve points for resourcefulness, if nothing else. Their regimen: bathing in tubs filled with donkey milk—adding some perfumed swan's fat for that special touch.

WHOEVER COINED THE TERM
honeymoon WAS NO ROMANTIC.

Have you ever wondered how the term *honeymoon* got its name? The word first began to appear in the 16th century, and, despite its romantic aura, it has a dark side. The *honey* part, as you might expect, is a reference to the sweetness of a new marriage. But the *moon* has nothing to do with dancing in the moonlight. It's an acknowledgment that the sweetness, just like a full moon, eventually diminishes.

"The way to love anything is to realize that it might be lost."

G.K. CHESTERTON

CRIMINALS HATE VALENTINES.

There's no good reason that even a criminal wouldn't
enjoy receiving a birthday card or Christmas card.
But a valentine would be most unwelcome.
In criminal jargon, "getting a valentine" means
receiving a one-year jail sentence.

30

MONEY CAN'T BUY LOVE, BUT THERE
WAS A TIME WHEN TOBACCO COULD.

When the English first settled in Jamestown, they had
to establish many societal rules to help govern
themselves. This included establishing the proper
dowry a man needed to pay for a new bride.
After careful deliberation, a sum was agreed on: 120
pounds—and not British monetary pounds.
Pounds of tobacco.

ROMANCE OUT-ROCKS A ROCK.

In a nationwide poll, more than 2,000 Americans were asked which was more important when it comes to popping the question: a huge diamond or a romantic proposal. Despite what all the ads for various jewelry stores would indicate, an overwhelming 87 percent said that a romantic proposal was more important than a big rock.

"I never hated
a man enough
to give him
his diamonds back."

ZSA ZSA GABOR

SOMETIMES, LOVE MEANS
GIVING THE FINGER.

If you visit New Guinea, you might notice some of
the elderly natives sporting less than a full set of
fingers. The reason? Many years ago, it was customary
for a young fighting man to give his girlfriend a finger
cut from the hand of an opponent. The girlfriend
would then proudly wear the battle trophy
on a string around her neck.

A KISS IS NOT JUST A KISS,
AT LEAST IN GERMANY.

The English language has its share of synonyms for
a kiss: smooch, smack, and peck, among others.
But the German language contains no fewer than 30
words for the act of kissing. And just to show how
fluent they are in this subject, the Germans even
have a word—*nachkuss*   for all the kisses that
haven't yet been named.

34

A GREAT ACTING PART
IS A LABOR OF LOVE.

Legends abound about actors falling in love with their co-stars, but performers can fall in love with a part as well as a player. When Kate Winslet finished reading the script for the film *Titanic,* she knew immediately she had to play the role of Rose. She phoned director James Cameron and informed him that he "would be mad" not to cast her opposite Leonardo DiCaprio, whom she deemed a genius actor.

When DiCaprio began to waver about playing the part of Jack, Winslet cornered him at his hotel in Cannes and pleaded her case. Winslet and DiCaprio became fast friends. And the movie became a mega-hit.

35

TAKE TWO CHOCOLATES
AND CALL ME IN THE MORNING...

In the 1800s, physicians sometimes prescribed an
interesting medicine for their patients suffering
from lovesickness: chocolate. The doctors claimed
that eating chocolate could cure one's
love-inflicted pining.

*"All I really need
is love,
but a little chocolate
now and then
doesn't hurt."*

LUCY VAN PELT (PEANUTS)

WHEN IT COMES TO FLAVORS, CHOCOLATE IS AMERICA'S FIRST LOVE.

Despite all of the exotic flavors available today,
Americans love chocolate best. In a nationwide
survey, 52 percent put chocolate at the top of the list.
(Vanilla was a distant second, at 12 percent.)
This preference is born out in U.S. eating habits.
Per capita, Americans eat an average of 11 pounds
of chocolate annually. That's the equivalent of 100
chocolate bars per person.

37

LOVE MAY BE FOREVER,
BUT DIAMONDS ARE NOT.

Don't believe all of those promises about a diamond
being forever—and therefore the quintessential
gift of love. While diamonds, made of pure carbon,
are renowned for being one of the hardest and most
durable substances known to humanity, they do
sublime at high temperatures. That is, at a temperature
of 3,500 degrees Celsius, a diamond will turn
directly from a solid to a gas.

LOVE IS CUCKOO FOR COCOA.

Cocoa beans played an important part in early Mayan
social and religious customs. At a wedding,
for example, the bride gave the bridegroom a small,
colorfully painted stool and five cocoa beans.
In return, the groom gave his bride several new
skirts—and another five cocoa beans.

"It is not
that chocolates
are a substitute
for love.
Love is a substitute
for chocolate.
Chocolate is,
let's face it,
far more reliable
than a man."

MIRANDA INGRAM

ALASKA: THE STATE WHERE IT'S RAINING *(snowing)* MEN.

While the general U.S. population contains more eligible women than men, things are different up north—way up north. With the highest ratio of unmarried men to unmarried women in the country, Alaska seems like an ideal place for a woman to find a mate. But the pickings might not be as good as they seem. As the local saying goes, "The odds are good, but the goods are odd."

LOVE CAN PRESENT
KING-SIZED DILEMMAS.

If you had to choose between your mate and your
favorite snack, what would you do? Such was the
dilemma of Maria Theresa of Spain when she married
Louis XIV of France. Maria brought with her a
following of servants from Madrid. These women,
like Maria, were devoted chocolate drinkers.
(For about 90 percent of its history, chocolate has
been enjoyed primarily as a beverage.) However,
the king proclaimed that consuming chocolate
was not something that "proper Frenchwomen"
indulged in. Faced with sacrificing her chocolate or
risking Louis' wrath, Maria and her servants settled
on a compromise. They found a way to indulge their
chocolate cravings in secret. There is no record that
King Louis ever caught them.

CUPID IS KINDEST TO KIDS, NOT ADULTS.

The box of chocolates for one's sweetheart is a staple among Valentine's Day gifts, but it's kids who receive the most goodies on February 14. Mom/wife comes in second, followed by dad/husband, grandparents, and pets.

CHOCOLATE CAN BE A GIFT FROM THE HEART AND *for* THE HEART.

There's a new buzzword in the discussion
of good health: phenols. Phenols are organic
compounds that inhibit clots by thinning the blood.
Thinner blood, of course, is easier for the heart to
pump throughout the body, so phenols can help
reduce the risk of heart attack. And, as a true
chocolate lover could tell you, a dark-chocolate bar
offers ten times more phenols than an orange
and four times more than a serving of beets.

As with all things, moderation is the key. About 1.5
ounces of dark chocolate a day is a recommended
"dosage." This serving size will give you about
the same amount of heart-healthy phenols
as drinking a glass and a half of red wine.

WHEN IT COMES TO WHITE WEDDINGS, IT'S HARD TO TOP FRANCES CLEVELAND.

Celebrities can brag about their posh weddings, but they have nothing on Frances Cleveland. She was the first bride of a U.S. president to be married in the White House. And when 21-year-old Frances married Grover Cleveland in 1886, she also became the youngest first lady. And she wasn't done making history. In 1893, she gave birth to Esther Cleveland, the only child ever born to a first lady in the White House.

THE ODDEST ODD COUPLE
ISN'T HUMAN.

Generally, when you see a small rodent in a cage
with a snake, it's because the former is the
dinner and the latter is the diner. But this is not the
case for Gohan, a hamster, and Aochan, a rat snake,
both residents at Japan's Mutsugoro Okoku Zoo.
Gohan is the Japanese word for "meal," which was
the hamster's intended role when he was placed
in Aochan's cage. However, the two critters quickly
became good friends—and have remained so.
Sometimes Gohan even climbs on
Aochan's back to take a nap.

ALL TRUE LOVERS ARE AMATEURS.

Being called an amateur in the ways of love isn't really an insult. The word *amateur* comes from the Latin *amator,* which means "a lover." And, unlike its connotations today, the original spirit of the word reflected motive more than expertise. In the purest sense, an amateur engaged in something—a craft, a sport, or even romance—for the pure love of it, as opposed to money or prestige. So the next time someone calls you an amateur, just smile and say, "Thank you."

"In love, as in other matters, the young are just beginners."

ISAAC BASHEVIS SINGER

46

THE EXISTENCE OF SPANISH FLY
IS A MYTH . . . SORT OF.

"Spanish Fly" (a medicinal mixture of dried beetles)
is legendary for its aphrodisiac properties. There's
just one problem. Technically speaking, there
is no such thing as a Spanish fly. A Spanish fly is
actually a pyrochroid beetle, which produces a
substance called cantharidin. This substance isn't a
love-enhancer, but as it irritates the urogenital tract,
it can produce physical results similar to those of
drugs like Viagra. In the insect kingdom, cantharidin
has a more important function. The female
pyrochroid beetle obtains the substance from the
male, and then passes it on to her eggs, since it makes
them less tasty to predators like ladybugs.

SCIENCE + LOVE
CAN BE ONE WEIRD MIX.

Nikola Tesla will go down in history as one
of the world's keenest scientific minds. He's the man
behind alternating current and, of course, the
famous Tesla coil. He even won some technical
debates with Thomas Edison. On the personal side,
though, Tesla's life was less than electric. He was an
obsessive hand-washer and staunchly despised round
objects. But greater than his hatred for round things
was his love for pigeons. (Yes, pigeons.)

He was so enamored of one particular pigeon that
when it died, he wrote, "Yes, I loved her as a man
loves a woman, and she loved me. . . . When that
pigeon died, something went out of my life. . . .
I knew my life's work was over."

"Love,
love,
love,
that is the soul
of genius."

WOLFGANG AMADEUS MOZART

48

WHEN YOU'RE A
PRINCESS ACTRESS, YOU DON'T NEED
THE PROPS DEPARTMENT.

The 1956 movie *High Society* marked Grace Kelly's
exit from the acting life, as she retired from film to
play her most important role—wife of Prince
Rainier of Monaco. And to demonstrate that she had
no second thoughts about leaving Hollywood behind,
Grace wore her huge diamond engagement ring
throughout the film (which costarred Bing Crosby).

49

A KISS BEATS A CAR
CHASE ANY DAY.

Steve McQueen was king of the high-speed
car-chase flick, as demonstrated in films like *Bullitt*
and *The Getaway*. But his personal favorite was
The Thomas Crown Affair, a somewhat more subdued,
psychologically driven movie. It's rumored that part
of McQueen's affection for the film was the kissing
scene with costar Faye Dunaway. That minute-long
scene took about eight hours to film
over the course of several days.

MY EXPENSIVE VALENTINE . . .

Valentine's Day might not seem like an expensive
gift-giving holiday when compared to Christmas,
but the average American digs pretty deep into his or
her pocket every February 14—and spends something
to the tune of $112.62 on presents.
(And that's not including cards, dinner, etc.)
Where does that hundred bucks (and then some) go?

Here's the breakdown:

Gifts for spouse/significant other: $80.29

Gifts for family members: $25.00

Gifts for friends: $4.93

Gifts for coworkers: $2.40

51

LOVE WILL PROTECT YOU—
AT LEAST IF YOU'RE A MOTH.

People aren't the only creatures that use protection during sexual activity. One species of red moth uses protection, too. But not protection against pregnancy—protection of life itself. The male moth dines on dog-fennel leaves and stores some of the plant's fluid contents in pouches under his abdomen. Then, when he finds a female moth to court, he releases the pouches' contents on the object of his desire. The female is grateful for the little shower, as the fluids repel predators such as spiders. In fact, in experiments, moths coated in this substance and then placed in spiders' webs were released unharmed by their arachnid captors.

NO MAN IS AN ISLAND, BUT LOVE CAN MAKE A MAN BUY AN ISLAND.

While filming *Mutiny on the Bounty,* screen legend Marlon Brando fell in love. Twice. Once with the delightful islands of Tahiti and then with his beautiful 19-year-old Polynesian costar Tarita Teriipia. The two were married the same year the film was released (1962). And just to prove it wasn't "all about the girl," Brando bought his own 150-acre Tahitian island as well.

"Love does not dominate; it cultivates."

GOETHE

THE NAKED TRUTH ABOUT
LADY GODIVA . . .

Nearly everyone knows that Lady Godiva rode
horseback through Coventry, England "clothed only
in chastity." But not as many know why. Lady Godiva's
husband, Earl Leofric, is to blame (or thank,
depending on how you look at it). Lady Godiva was
distressed about an oppressive tax on the poor, and
she begged the Earl to abolish it. He agreed, but only
if his wife would ride unclothed through the town.
Paradoxically, the Earl ordered the townspeople not
to look at her as she did. Clearly, the Earl had
issues. Too bad he lived about a thousand
years before Dr. Phil.

BOGART AND BERGMAN: WERE THEY OR WEREN'T THEY?

For decades, rumors abounded that Humphrey Bogart and his *Casablanca* costar Ingrid Bergman had an affair that was sparked during the filming of the classic film. However, when the picture's 60th anniversary was celebrated, family members of both stars noted that Bogey and Bergman didn't get along during filming. Bergman's daughter, Isabella Rossellini, went so far as to say that the two "weren't even friends," much less lovers.

However, despite all the evidence to the contrary, some movie buffs still witness the undeniable on-screen chemistry and wonder, "Could that really be faked?"

"A kiss
is a lovely trick
designed by nature
to stop speech
when words
become superfluous.

INGRID BERGMAN

HAPPY COUPLES BRING
HOME THE BACON.

In old England, "bringing home the bacon" had
nothing to do with earning a living—and everything
to do with a happy marriage. Couples who were
willing to swear upon the King James Bible that
they hadn't engaged in a marital spat in a year were
rewarded with a side of bacon. Trying to find a logical
connection between a hunk of cured pork and
marital bliss is like trying to catch a greased pig,
but then again, sometimes love defies logic.

SON OF A GUN!
THAT'S WHERE THAT
PHRASE CAME FROM?

The term "son of a gun" evokes a scene from
the Wild West, but its origin is actually nautical,
dating back to the early 1700s. During this era,
women were sometimes allowed to accompany their
sailor husbands at sea. Pregnancies soon followed
(shudder to think what it was like to experience
both morning sickness *and* seasickness!)
and it became common practice for a woman to give
birth beneath the guns of the ship. (Later, the phrase
"son of a gun" was expanded to include offspring
conceived illegitimately aboard a ship.)

KISS MY X!

Ever received a love letter with X's across the bottom? Using an X to designate a kiss dates clear back to medieval times, and it had nothing to do with romance. In an effort to show good intentions on contracts and other important documents, people placed an X after their signature. (X is a symbol for St. Andrew, one of Jesus' original 12 disciples, who, according to legend, was crucified on an X-shaped cross. As Andrew was a faithful disciple, his symbol was a sign of good faith.)

To deepen the significance of the pledge made in a document, the signee would kiss the X as a guarantee, noting, "I'll faithfully fulfill my obligation."

58

THE COUPLE THAT
GOLFS TOGETHER . . .

In 1997, the winnings of an LPGA Tour hole-in-one
pool were promised to the caddie of the golfer who
scored an ace. At that year's U.S. Women's Open,
Susie Redman carded a hole in one during the first
round, earning her caddie $1,700. Ms. Redman was
especially happy for her caddie, who happened
to be her husband, Bo.

*"Happiness
makes its home
in hearts
filled with love."*

LUCY VAN PELT (PEANUTS)

"NOT TONIGHT, HONEY, I'M ALLERGIC TO YOU."

A person can be allergic to anything, including one's spouse. One woman suddenly became allergic to her husband—after 25 years of marriage. As soon as this unfortunate hubby came home from work, his wife started experiencing allergy symptoms: breathing problems and various aches and pains. Desperate, the couple lived apart for months while doctors searched for the source of the problem.

Fortunately, they eventually cracked the case. The husband was a dentist, and his practice had switched to a new type of anesthetic, which triggered his wife's allergies. Thorough showers for the DDS, coupled with a change of clothes before he went home, brought an end to the wife's allergies— and the resumption of marital bliss.

BEER GOGGLES FOR COCKROACHES?

Scientists have discovered that female cockroaches, like their human counterparts, will lower their standards for a mate when their biological clock begins to tick. Observers noted that female cockroaches became less selective in their search for Mr. Right Cockroach as their reproductive potential decreased. The male cockroaches, on the other hand, showed no difference in behavior, regardless of the age or fertility of the female.

BEING THE BRIDE OF FRANKENSTEIN IS A TALL ORDER.

If you've ever seen the classic 1935 horror film *Bride of Frankenstein,* perhaps you've marveled at the height of Elsa Lanchester, who played the title role. In reality, Elsa was only about five-foot-four, so she spent the entire film trussed to a pair of stilts to make her seven feet tall, and able to see eye-to-eye with costar Boris Karloff, who achieved his monstrous height via massive lifts placed in his shoes.

Ms. Lanchester proved more agile on her stilts than Karloff in his lifts, since he stumbled into a well during filming and broke his leg. Ah, the things monsters do for love . . . .

"Love is the greatest beautifier in the universe."

MAY CHRISTIE

HAPPY VALENTINE'S DAY—
AND WATCH OUT FOR WOLVES!

Some authorities say that Valentine's Day actually
predates either of the saints who bore the name
Valentine. These authorities trace the holiday's roots
back to an ancient Roman festival called Lupercalia,
which was held on February 15. Its purpose?
To ensure protection from wolves. During this
festival, young men struck various people with strips
of animal hide, as conventional wisdom of the time
held that flogging by animal hide was the ideal wolf
repellant. Women were typically the (willing!)
recipients, since they believed that the beatings,
in addition to warding off wolves, would
also make them more fertile.

ON CELEBRITY MARRIAGES
AND OTHER SHORT SUBJECTS . . .

Everyone knows that some celebrities change
marriage partners about as often as they change
socks, but not everyone knows just how short
some celebrity marriages can be.

Britney Spears' Las Vegas hook-up with childhood
pal Jason Alexander was annulled just 55 hours
after they exchanged vows, but actress Robin Givens
humbles Ms. Spears in the quick-to-the-alter,
quick-to-falter department. Her marriage to her
tennis coach, Svetozar Marinkovic, lasted but a
day—making her 11-month relationship with Mike
Tyson seem like a lifetime by comparison.

In the future, Spears and Givens could face competi-
tion from Drew Barrymore, whose two failed
marriages (so far) have averaged about 84 days each.

"A woman's
got to love
a bad man
once or twice
in her life
to be thankful for
a good one."

MARJORIE KINNAN RAWLINGS

DYING TO MATE

People might complain, "If I don't find a spouse soon, I'm gonna die!" But if ferrets could talk, they'd have every right to make this statement. Female ferrets go into heat during the first spring season of their lives and remain in heat until they are successfully mated. If mating doesn't occur, they will succumb to aplastic anemia and die a painful death. For this reason, if you give your loved one a female ferret for Valentine's Day (or any other reason) you should have it spayed. This increases a ferret's life span—and reduces the power of that pungent ferret odor.

65

From the mid 1800s to the early 1900s, before the
days of Hallmark cards, many people sent comic
valentines called "penny dreadfuls."
These cards cost a penny
and featured rather insulting verses.
How insulting? Here's one example:

'Tis all in vain your simpering looks
You never can incline,
With all your bustles, stays, and curls,
To find a valentine.

Suffice it to say, the most successful suitors
chose not to make the penny dreadful
part of their Valentine's Day repertoire.

MAKING UP FOR LOST TIME

Resting up for a big romantic encounter is a good idea, but the cicada takes this principle to the extreme. Some species of these insects hibernate underground for up to 17 years before finally awaking and emerging to mate. The male cicada plays a love song to a potential mate using a pair of ribbed membranes on his abdomen. Some varieties of cicada sing at 120 decibels, which is the pain threshold for the human ear. Others sing in a pitch so high that it's beyond the range of human hearing.

Once a male wins a female's heart through song, the two mate. The female lays her eggs and Mr. and Mrs. Cicada die. But in another 17 years, their children will emerge to carry on the family name.

A DANISH VALENTINE MYSTERY

In Denmark, some Danish men send valentines called *gaekkebrevs* (or joking letters). The sender composes a rhyme for the object of his affection, but he doesn't reveal his name. Instead, he "signs" the valentine with a dot for each letter of his name. If the woman who receives the mystery correspondence can guess the identity of the sender, he rewards her. But not with a date or marriage proposal—with an egg on the following Easter.

"At the touch
of love,
everyone becomes
a poet."

PLATO

MONKEY LOVE SONNETS?

You've probably heard the hypothesis: Give a
million monkeys a million typewriters—and a million
years—and they could produce a love sonnet or some
other Shakespearean work, purely by chance.

It sounds somewhat plausible—after all, we're
talking about a lot of monkeys and a lot of time.
British researchers, however, wanted to explore the
idea further. They gave six short-tailed monkeys
a computer, then sat back to watch them "compose."

The result: Some of the monkeys did hit a few
keystrokes, mostly long strings of S's. But for the
most part, they used the machine for other
purposes. They defecated on it, urinated on it, and
beat it with rocks. But don't we all feel that way
about our computers sometimes?

69

SOMETIMES, IT'S NOT SO GOOD
TO BE THE QUEEN.

Marrying young has its challenges, whether you're
Britney Spears or the queen of France. Marie
Antoinette married at age 14 and assumed the role of
France's queen (in 1774) at only 19. Her lavish lifestyle
earned her the nickname "Madam Deficit" from her sub-
jects, and her infamous line ("Let them eat cake!")
didn't do much for her popularity, either.

After the French Revolution, the monarchy
crumbled, and King Louis XVI was guillotined
in January of 1793. Several months later,
Marie herself met the same fate.

THE SWEETEST DAY: WHAT IS IT?

Valentine's Day hogs most of the headlines, but those
savvy in the lore of love know about another day
devoted to all things *amore*. Sweetest Day, celebrated
on the third Saturday of October, was established in
the 1920s by a Cleveland candy company employee
who wanted to bring happiness to orphans,
the elderly, and others who were often forgotten.
In the years that followed, the day evolved into a time
for connecting with loved ones and friends.
Nationwide, about 1.5 million Sweetest Day cards
are exchanged each year, along with candy,
flowers, and small gifts.

"To see a young couple
loving each other
is no wonder,
but to see an old couple
loving each other
is the best sight of all."

WILLIAM MAKEPEACE THACKERAY

NOTE TO BACHELORS:
STAY OUT OF QATAR!

It's said that there's a woman for every man, but in
the emirate of Qatar, it's simply not true. Qatar has
the worst male-to-female ratio (from a guy's
perspective, that is) of any country in the world.
There are 2.36 eligible men for every woman, which
puts Qatar well ahead of Kuwait (in second
place with 1.77 men for every woman)
and Samoa (with 1.68).

THE TEN SWEETEST
HONEYMOON SPOTS

It's probably no surprise that, according to CNN's
Web site, Hawaii is the most popular honeymoon
destination. (In fact, our 50th state has held that
honor for the past nine years running.) But how many
of the other top ten can you name? (And please don't
guess Qatar!) Give up? Here's the rest of the best . . .

2. *Italy*

3. *Tahiti*

4. *Anguilla*

5. *Fiji*

6. *St. Lucia*

7. *Mexico*

8. *St. Barths*

9. *Jamaica*

10. *France*

73

TEENS KNOW A LOT ABOUT LOVE.
Despite the superficial depictions of teens on
television dramas and sit-coms—and the spoiled,
hormonal specimens selected for MTV reality
shows—most teenagers who live in the real world
show remarkable insight and good intentions on the
subject of love. Here's a sampling of quotes from
teens nationwide, in response to the question, "What
is love?"

"Love is wanting the utmost for somebody else."
JOHN, 16

"Love is unconditional forgiving, even when it's hard."
NICK, 14

"Love is a gift from God for all of us to share."
CHRISTIE, 15

"Love is having the willingness to sacrifice."
TONY, 14

"Love is dying for somebody."
AARON, 16

ANIMAL ATTRACTION

Did you know only three percent of about 4,000 mammal species mate for life? Among them are wolves, barn owls, beavers, bald eagles, and termites.

Then again, it depends on what one means by "mate for life." Several species do, in a social sense, by living in pairs and raising children. But they are rarely 100 percent faithful.

The anglerfish, on the other hand, is absolutely, positively monogamous. The tiny male fish finds his beloved by scent, then holds onto her with his teeth. Soon, the two fishes fuse together—literally. (Talk about needing some space!)

CUPID VERSUS SAINT ANDREW

Cupid isn't the only resource one can turn to for help in winning the heart of that special someone. Near midnight on November 29 (the day before Saint Andrew's Day), it is traditional for young Scottish women to pray to Saint Andrew for a husband.

For a sign that her petition to the saint has been heard, she can do one of two things:

1. Throw a shoe at a door in her home. If the toe of the shoe points toward the exit, it is a sign that the young woman will marry and leave her home within a year.

2. Peel a whole apple rind and toss it over her shoulder. If the rind forms a letter of the alphabet, it will be the first initial of her future groom.

These traditions might seem odd, but, then again, so is the notion of a bow-and-arrow-wielding little guy in a diaper.

SO WHY THE ♥, ANYWAY?

Ever wonder why the heart is a symbol for love—
and not another vital organ? Long ago, people
believed that all emotions, from fear to excitement to
joy, were housed in the heart. As time went on, they
reasoned that most of the various emotions actually
resided in the brain. By process of elimination, they
came to the conclusion that the only true "emotion
of the heart" was love.

"Since love
          grows within you,
so beauty grows.
For love is the beauty
          of the soul."

St. Augustine

LOVE ON THE JOB

Americans love a lot of things: their families, their
pets, their vehicles, and their home teams. But one
thing they are not loving so much lately are their
J-O-Bs. U.S. job satisfaction has been declining
steadily over the past 20 years, according to a recent
USA Today survey of 5,000 U.S. households.

Back in 1987, 61 percent of Americans said they
were satisfied with their jobs. By the year 2000, that
number dwindled to 51 percent, and in 2006, it
dipped below the 50-percent mark. For that year,
only 47 percent could say they were satisfied with
their life at work.

CASANOVA'S SECRET

Infamous Italian writer—and womanizer—Casanova used chocolate as his go-to romance potion. He said that he found chocolate "more stimulating than champagne." And he would know. He boasted of having affairs with 122 women.

Casanova's French contemporary, the Marquis De Sade, was also convinced of chocolate's erotic powers. Even when he was imprisoned (for his various cruelties to women), he wrote to his long-suffering wife, begging for chocolate. She obliged, and he grew grossly obese during his long imprisonment. When he was finally released, his wife decided she'd suffered long enough and promptly divorced him. (Smart move. Who would want to stay married to the guy who gave sadism its name?)

IN THE BIBLE, NOT ALL LOVE IS CREATED EQUAL.

The word *love* doesn't always mean the same thing.
The Greek language, for instance, offers several words
that translate to "love" in English. For example, *philia*
refers to "brotherly love," the kind shared between family
and friends. (Philadelphia is, literally, the
City of Brotherly Love.)

Eros, on the other hand, is romantic or sexual love.
Hence the English word *erotic.*

There is also *agape,* which is more spiritual—and
somewhat more complicated—than romance.
The famous wedding reading beginning, "Love is patient,
love is kind" is talking about *agape.*

"Above all,
love each other
deeply,
because love
covers over
a multitude
of sins."

SAINT PETER

THE POMPATUS OF LOVE

The Steve Miller Band's 1973 hit "The Joker" contains one of the most misquoted lyrics in all of pop music. Some people swear that early in the song Miller sings of *the hippopotamus of love*—raising the question, "What, exactly, *is* the hippopotamus of love?"

Actually, it's *pompatus,* but that doesn't make things any clearer. That's because the word *pompatus* isn't a real word. It's a variant of yet another made-up phrase: *puppetutes of love.*

The 1954 Medallions song "The Letter" refers to a *puppetute,* a paper-doll fantasy figure that can fulfill a man's every desire. Miller tried to borrow the line for his song, but somehow came up with *pompatus* instead.

(Maybe that's why some called him "The Space Cowboy.")

81

LOOKING FOR LOVE?
DON'T TRY THESE LINES!

The Internet has become a promising pool for catching the love of one's life. But as with any other online prospect, one must be wary. One way to weed out the bottom-feeders is to look for schmaltz or lack of originality in people's online profiles. Here are the five worst ones, according to *Online Dating Magazine*:

1. I might be the one you're looking for!

2. Hi! (See also: "Hello!" "Howdy!" and "Hey there!")

3. Seeking Prince Charming

4. I'm the one your mother warned you about.

5. I can't believe I'm doing this!

ONE HUNNY OF A HONEYMOON!

On his wedding night, the infamous 5th-century warrior Atilla the Hun got so drunk that he didn't realize it when his nose began to bleed profusely at some point in the honeymoon proceedings. Mrs. Hun (real name: Idico) awoke the next morning to find her new groom dead, drowned in his own blood.

"They say women love a man in uniform. It's true. The uniform sends a clear message: He has a job."

MIMI GONZALEZ

DEARLY BELOVED, WHERE DID THE PHRASE "DEARLY BELOVED" COME FROM?

How many times have you heard a wedding ceremony begin with "Dearly beloved, we are gathered together . . ."?

Some people think this phrasing comes from the Bible, but it's actually the beginning of the traditional wedding ceremony, as found in older editions of *The Book of Common Prayer,* which contains the official liturgy of the Anglican churches.

This little volume boasts lots of greatest hits, including " to have and to hold" and "for better or for worse."

KIDS KNOW LOVE.

Ask a bunch of kids what love is, and you get a variety
of answers, but there is a thread that connects them
all. Read on and see for yourself.

"Love is . . . Daddy!"
BRYCE, AGE 8

*"Being in love means you let your husband
see your fat jiggle."*
LILLY, AGE 11

*"Love is when your parents willn't be mad
at you when you make a mistake."*
CARRIE, AGE 4

"Love is letting Grandma pinch your cheeks."
TRENT, AGE 8

*"Love is when your mommy sits in the bathroom
with you when you are getting sick,
and she doesn't get mad when you throw up on her."*
AARON, AGE 6

BEFORE YOU KISS YOUR DOG . . .

Americans love their dogs—all 75 million of them.
However, among the many ways to show a dog your
affection, smooching him or her isn't the best
idea—despite the old adage about a dog's mouth
being cleaner than a human's. Like many adages, that
one isn't true. Yes, the average human mouth harbors
37 types of bacteria, but a dog's mouth has 53.

So the next time you want to show your dog some
love, try a warm hug, a tummy rub,
or a good old game of fetch.

PARENTS AND KIDS:
WHERE'S THE LOVE?

It seems that American kids could use a lot more love
from their parents. Want evidence? Supposedly, the
average parent spends six hours a week shopping,
but only 40 minutes a week with his or her kid(s).
That's 40 percent less shared time than in 1965—
and 50 percent less than in 1960.

Some parents might complain that life has become
busier and more complicated over the past four-plus
decades, but in reality, thanks to increased technology
and convenience, Americans enjoy an hour more of
daily free time than their 1965 counterparts.

"The hunger
for love
is more difficult
to feed
than the hunger
for bread."

MOTHER TERESA

THE IDEAL AGE FOR
MARRIAGE IS _____ ?

American men and women are getting married later
in life—about seven years later than they did in the
1950s. Today, the average age for a first marriage
is 29 for men and 27 for women.

But what does today's younger generation think about
the "whens and whys" of marriage? Here are some
of their answers:

"I want to get married at 30, because, I hope,
I'll be mentally stable by then."

NICK, AGE 14

"Hey, I want to get married whenever
Miss Right comes along."

AARON, AGE 16

"I want to get married when I'm 30, because
maybe by then the guys my age will grow up."

COURTNEY, AGE 15

RHINO HORN —THE ULTIMATE LOVE POTION?

For centuries, people (especially men) have ingested various animals, vegetables, and minerals in the search of the ultimate love potion.

A current fad is extract of rhino horn, which you might find on the shelves of your local drug store. But while a rhino is impressively large and powerful, ingesting its horn is the ultimate act of futility. You see, a rhino's horn is really just a dense, hard-packed compound of hair and keratin—the stuff your fingernails are made of. So, you'd do just as well to chew your hair and bite your nails. The effect on your libido will be the same, and you'll help save the rhino, which is endangered.

TCHAIKOVSKY'S SUGAR MAMA

If you've ever thrilled to the sounds of ballets like *Swan Lake, Sleeping Beauty,* and *The Nutcracker,* you can thank the brilliance of Peter Tchaikovsky, the Russian composer. But you should also thank Nadezhda von Meck, the woman who helped make the romantic music possible—but not in the way you might think.

The wealthy widow was so moved by Tchaikovsky's music that she sent him a monthly allowance so that he could dedicate himself to composing. And just to show that she had no hidden agenda, Ms. Von Meck stipulated as part of the deal that she and Tchaikovsky were never to meet.

To show his appreciation to his benefactor, Tchaikovsky dedicated his Fourth Symphony to Von Meck, with the words "To My Best Friend."

IS A KISS JUST A KISS?

According to scientists, no. Not really. And anyone who's ever been kissed knows there's much more to it than just puckering up. But what, exactly?

During a kiss, nerves carry sensations from the lips to the brain. The brain (that sly fellow) responds by releasing a love potion of sorts—a mixture of biochemicals. The first is oxytocin, known for its role in developing feelings of affection and attachment. The second, dopamine, processes the feeling of pleasure. The third ingredient, seratonin, elevates the mood. And adrenalin, the fourth and final ingredient, increases the heart rate. But what sets those butterflies aflight in the stomach? Well, that's still a mystery.

CARRYING SUPERSTITION ACROSS
THE THRESHOLD

Ever wonder why it's customary for the groom to carry his bride across the threshold of their home, apartment, or honeymoon suite?

This superstition comes from Scotland, where, long ago, witches were believed to place curses on newlyweds' thresholds, causing the bride to trip and fall as she crossed. This mishap would launch a lifetime of marital misfortune and misery.

Fortunately, the curse could be thwarted by a gallant groom hoisting his love into the air, carrying her across the doorsill, and depositing her safely inside the house.

THE BALD TRUTH ABOUT
THE FRANZ LISZT GROUPIES . . .

Franz Liszt (1811–1886) was a concert pianist by age
12, and soon the virtuoso was traveling throughout
Europe, creating a sensation wherever he went. In
some ways, he was the first-ever rock star. The term
Lisztomania was coined during his lifetime, as women
often swooned during his performance.

And the women did more than swoon. Liszt received
so many requests for a lock of his hair that he realized
he would be perpetually bald keeping up with the
demand. So he bought a dog and began snipping off
chunks of its fur to send to his many female admirers.

*"Love is an
irresistible desire
to be irresistibly desired."*

ROBERT FROST

UNDER THE MISTLETOE

If you've ever stolen a kiss under the mistletoe, thank the Druids. They believed the mistletoe plant to be a symbol of peace, so the politically tenuous negotiations between warring Celtic tribes were held under branches sporting these parasitic plants.

During Christmastime, the season of peace and goodwill, people began hanging mistletoe over doorways, where guests were often greeted with a friendly kiss, or "holy kiss." And during the 18th century in England, it became permissible for an unmarried man to kiss any unmarried woman whom he happened to catch standing beneath it.

Incidentally, while kissing under mistletoe can be enjoyable, don't try to eat it. Both its berries and leaves are toxic and potentially lethal to humans and pets.

94

FOR THE LOVE OF THE GAME

Usually, the only thing stolen in a baseball game is a
base or two, but for more than 20 years, an unusual
baseball fan became famous for stealing something
else: kisses. Morganna, an extremely buxom blond
known as "The Kissing Bandit," was so enamored with
professional baseball players that she used to trot
onto the field and plant a smooch on her favorites.
She managed to deliver a smacker to Kansas City
superstar George Brett during the 1979 All Star Game.

Morganna didn't stop kissing until 1999. Probably
because, by this time, she was no longer agile enough
to elude stadium security measures.

95

Many of the antiquated laws still on the books in some states involve the proper treatment of the animal kingdom. For example, in Tennessee it's still illegal to use a lasso to catch a fish. And don't even think about bothering a butterfly in Pacific Grove, California. You'll be subject to a $500 fine.

While laws like these must have sprung from the desire to protect various critters, there's a law in Idaho that must have been dreamed up by either a confectioners union or some chocolate-loving women. In the Potato State, it's illegal for a man to give his wife or girlfriend a box of candy weighing less than 50 pounds.

"My weaknesses
    have always been
food and men,
    in that order."

DOLLY PARTON

SEE A MAGPIE, GET MARRIED?

It's not one of the most popular superstitions,
but perhaps you've heard the one where a magpie
sighting meant a man or woman would find a mate.

This superstition springs from a Chinese legend
involving an emperor's daughter who fell in love with
a cowherd. The emperor, wanting his daughter to find
a more socially acceptable mate than a lowly tender
of livestock, exiled the lovers to opposite ends of the
sky—and ordered a band of stars to keep them apart.

Fortunately for the couple, a flock of magpies took
pity on the princess and her cowherd, and they built
an enchanted bridge so that the couple could make
their way to each other accross the sky.

ARE YOU AN AILUROPHILE?

If you are, indeed, an ailurophile, you're not alone.
America is full of them.

An ailurophile is someone who loves cats. And many
Americans really, really love their cats. In fact, 67
percent of the 88 million cats in the U.S. get to sleep
in bed with their owners. Almost 40 percent get
Christmas presents. All told, cat owners spend about
$1,000 a year on each of their furry friends.

By the way, according to some animal behaviorists,
if your cat loves you back, he or she will gaze at you
through half-closed eyes. (This, however, is probably
not a sign of affection from your human
significant other.)

WEDDING ETIQUETTE:
TO TOSS RICE OR NOT?

If you've been to a wedding recently, perhaps you have been given a small, politically correct packet of birdseed—instead of rice—to toss at the bride and groom. The explanation: wild birds cannot digest rice. "The grains will puff up in a bird's stomach," you might have heard, "and the poor creature will explode!"

The truth, however, is that no wedding-goers have ever reported sightings of exploding birds in the vicinity. Why not? As any ornithologist or rice-grower could tell you, wild birds feed in rice fields all the time. Rice eaten directly off the stalk doesn't kill them; neither do the grains they might find on the church steps.

CONGRATULATIONS ON YOUR MARRIAGE—AND WATCH OUT FOR THE DRIED PEAS!

Have you ever attended a wedding, stood outside with your handful of rice (or birdseed) and wondered what your counterparts in other parts of the world are flinging at the weddings they are attending?

*Here's a sampling of countries
and wedding projectiles of choice.*

Turkey: candy

Czech Republic: dried peas

North Africa: figs and dates

France: wheat

Mexico: red beads

Greece: candied almonds

Korea: nuts and dates

India: flower petals and puffed rice

Italy: coins, candy, and dried fruit

EQUALLY FERTILE GROUND?

For many couples, the quest to have children is an important but difficult one. About one couple in ten experiences fertility-related problems. Traditionally, many of the products designed to enhance the fertility process have been designed for women, but a new at-home screening test for men has been developed, and it allows men to measure their fertility in a little over an hour.

This development seems long overdue. About 40 percent of couples' fertility troubles are male-related compared to the 30 percent attributed to female factors. (The remaining 30 percent are medically unexplainable.)

AMERICANS STILL LOVE THEIR MOMS.

In the United States, more phone calls are made on Mother's Day than any other day of the year. (Father's Day, incidentally, is the number one day for collect phone calls.) What's more, about 150 million Mother's Day cards are exchanged nationwide—about double the number of Father's Day cards. (And about 70 percent of U.S. households celebrate both days.)

SOURCES

Editor's Note: This book's origins predate Google, Ask Jeeves, Wikipedia, and the like. In fact, when 101 Amazing Things About Love was begun, there was no Internet at all. Thus, many of the stories, legends, and figures of speech have been handed down by word of mouth, crossing generations and cultures. The editors and compilers have done their best to verify dates, names, quotes, and facts, but, like love itself, some entries remain shrouded in mystery, contradiction, and wonder. Perhaps that's as it should be. After all, this book wasn't created in the spirit of science or reference, but rather in the spirit of love.

That said, the following sources were helpful in verifying information and separating fact from fantasy:

Assorted Trifles, by Stanley Newman.
Published by Random House, 2005.

The Book of Love: The Farmer's Almanac Reconsiders Romance, Sex & Marriage,
by Christine Schultz. Published by Villard Press, 1996.

Captivating Couples (Hallmark Edition), by David Baird.
Published by MQ Publications Limited, 2005.

The Complete Book of Bible Knowledge, by Mark D. Taylor.
Published by Tyndale House Publishers, 1992.

Do Blue Bedsheets Bring Babies?, by Thomas Craughwell.
Published by Broadway Books, a division of Random House, Inc. 2005.

Fat, Dumb, and Ugly: The Decline of the Average American,
by Peter Strupp. Published by Simon & Schuster, 2004.

For the Love of Chocolate, by Cherie Rayburn.
Published by Gift Books from Hallmark, 2005.

A Little Book of Love, by Cherie Rayburn.
Published by Gift Books from Hallmark
in cooperation with Honor Books, 2002.

*In Love in Italy: A Traveler's Guide to the
Most Romantic Destinations in the Country of Amore*,
by Monica Larner. Published by Rizzoli, 2007.

mental_floss Magazine, various issues.

Movie Monsters (Hallmark Edition), by David Baird.
Published by MQ Publications Limited, 2005.

To a Child, Love Is Spelled T-I-M-E, by Mac Anderson and Lance Wubbels.
Published by Warner Faith, 2004.

The World's Worsts, by Les Krantz & Sue Sveum.
Published by HarperResource, a division of HarperCollins, 2005.

USA Today, various editions.

IF YOU HAVE ENJOYED THESE
101 AMAZING THINGS,
HALLMARK WOULD *love*
TO HEAR FROM YOU.

please send your comments to:

BOOK FEEDBACK
Hallmark Cards, Inc.
2501 McGee, Mail Drop 215
Kansas City, MO 64108

Or e-mail us at booknotes@hallmark.com.